Workout log

This log book belon

Name

Contact Info

Log book Info

Log Start date:

Log Number:

Designed and created using free resources from: pixabay.com, freepik.com, unsplash.com

Membership Details

Facility:	
Location:	
Contact Info:	
Account ID:	
Membership Info:	

Facility:	
Location:	
Contact Info:	
Account ID:	
Membership Info:	

My Goals

	Current	Target
Date		
Weight		
Body Fat		
Blood Pressure		
Resting heart rate		
Measurements		
Neck		
Shoulders		
Chest		
Waist		
Hips		
Upper Arm				
Forearm				
Thigh				
Calf				
Exercises		
Bench Press		
Squat		
Deadlift		
Overhead Press		
Barbell Row		

Weekly Workout Routine

Day	Exercise	Sets	Day	Exercise	Sets

Weekly Workout Routine

Day	Exercise	Sets	Day	Exercise	Sets

Weekly Workout Routine

Day	Exercise	Sets	Day	Exercise	Sets

Progress Tracker

Date				
Weight				
Body Fat				
Blood Pressure				
Resting heart rate				

Measurements

Neck				
Shoulders				
Chest				
Waist				
Hips				
Upper Arm								
Forearm								
Thigh								
Calf								

Exercises

Bench Press				
Squat				
Deadlift				
Overhead Press				
Barbell Row				

Progress Tracker

Measurements

Exercises

Date:	Start Time:				Finish Time:				
Mo Tu We Th Fr Sa Su	Workout:				Weight:				

Exercises	Set 1		Set 2		Set 3		Set 4		Set 5	
	Wt.	Rep	Wt.	Rep	Wt.	Rep	Wt.	Rep	Wt.	Rep

Comments:

Protein Intake | **Workout Rating** ★ ★ ★ ★ ★

Date:	Start Time:		Finish Time:	
Mo Tu We Th Fr Sa Su	Workout:		Weight:	

Exercises	Set 1		Set 2		Set 3		Set 4		Set 5	
	Wt.	Rep	Wt.	Rep	Wt.	Rep	Wt.	Rep	Wt.	Rep

Comments:

Protein Intake	Workout Rating ★ ★ ★ ★ ★

Date: 1/3/22	Start Time: 1.36		Finish Time: 1.40	

Mo Tu We Th Fr Sa Su | Workout: 5 | Weight:

Exercises	Set 1		Set 2		Set 3		Set 4		Set 5	
	Wt.	Rep	Wt.	Rep	Wt.	Rep	Wt.	Rep	Wt.	Rep
ASS pull	70	15	50	12	40	13				
Smith Shoulder	40	15	40	15	40	15				
Seated cable Fly	12.5	15	12.5	12	12c	15				
Rack pull 20Bar	80	15	50	12	80		full weight			
Arm cable	12.5	15	15	12	15	15				
Single Arm cable Lt	6.25	15	6.5	12	6.5	15 - sore	back			
Pin chest Press	40	15	45	12	40	13				
Arm curl machine	20	15	20	12	20	15				

Comments:

Ok just getting use to the
equipment + working out weight
working at 70%.

Protein Intake | **Workout Rating** ★ ★ ★ ★ ★

Date:	Start Time:			Finish Time:						
Mo Tu We Th Fr Sa Su	Workout:			Weight:						

Exercises	Set 1		Set 2		Set 3		Set 4		Set 5	
	Wt.	Rep	Wt.	Rep	Wt.	Rep	Wt.	Rep	Wt.	Rep

Comments:

Protein Intake

Workout Rating ★ ★ ★ ★ ★

Date:	Start Time:		Finish Time:	
Mo Tu We Th Fr Sa Su	Workout:		Weight:	

Exercises	Set 1		Set 2		Set 3		Set 4		Set 5	
	Wt.	Rep	Wt.	Rep	Wt.	Rep	Wt.	Rep	Wt.	Rep

Comments:

Protein Intake

Workout Rating ★ ★ ★ ★ ★

Date:	Start Time:				Finish Time:				
Mo Tu We Th Fr Sa Su	Workout:				Weight:				
Exercises	Set 1		Set 2		Set 3		Set 4		Set 5	
	Wt.	Rep	Wt.	Rep	Wt.	Rep	Wt.	Rep	Wt.	Rep

Comments:

Protein Intake

Workout Rating ★ ★ ★ ★ ★

Date:	Start Time:						Finish Time:				
Mo Tu We Th Fr Sa Su	Workout:						Weight:				
Exercises	Set 1		Set 2		Set 3		Set 4		Set 5		
	Wt.	Rep	Wt.	Rep	Wt.	Rep	Wt.	Rep	Wt.	Rep	

Comments:

Protein Intake

Workout Rating ★ ★ ★ ★ ★

Date:	Start Time:				Finish Time:				
Mo Tu We Th Fr Sa Su	Workout:				Weight:				

Exercises	Set 1		Set 2		Set 3		Set 4		Set 5	
	Wt.	Rep	Wt.	Rep	Wt.	Rep	Wt.	Rep	Wt.	Rep

Comments:

Protein Intake

Workout Rating ★ ★ ★ ★ ★

Date:	Start Time:		Finish Time:	
Mo Tu We Th Fr Sa Su	Workout:		Weight:	

Exercises	Set 1		Set 2		Set 3		Set 4		Set 5	
	Wt.	Rep	Wt.	Rep	Wt.	Rep	Wt.	Rep	Wt.	Rep

Comments:

Protein Intake	Workout Rating ★ ★ ★ ★ ★

Date:	Start Time:			Finish Time:					
Mo Tu We Th Fr Sa Su	Workout:			Weight:					

Exercises	Set 1		Set 2		Set 3		Set 4		Set 5	
	Wt.	Rep	Wt.	Rep	Wt.	Rep	Wt.	Rep	Wt.	Rep

Comments:

Protein Intake   **Workout Rating** ★ ★ ★ ★

Date:	Start Time:						Finish Time:				
Mo Tu We Th Fr Sa Su	Workout:						Weight:				

Exercises	Set 1		Set 2		Set 3		Set 4		Set 5	
	Wt.	Rep	Wt.	Rep	Wt.	Rep	Wt.	Rep	Wt.	Rep

Comments:

Protein Intake

Workout Rating ★ ★ ★ ★ ★

Date:	Start Time:					Finish Time:				
Mo Tu We Th Fr Sa Su	Workout:					Weight:				

Exercises	Set 1		Set 2		Set 3		Set 4		Set 5	
	Wt.	Rep	Wt.	Rep	Wt.	Rep	Wt.	Rep	Wt.	Rep

Comments:

Protein Intake	Workout Rating ★ ★ ★ ★ ★

Date:	Start Time:		Finish Time:	
Mo Tu We Th Fr Sa Su	Workout:		Weight:	

Exercises	Set 1		Set 2		Set 3		Set 4		Set 5	
	Wt.	Rep	Wt.	Rep	Wt.	Rep	Wt.	Rep	Wt.	Rep

Comments:

Protein Intake

Workout Rating ★ ★ ★ ★ ★

Date:		Start Time:			Finish Time:		
Mo Tu We Th Fr Sa Su		Workout:			Weight:		

Exercises	Set 1		Set 2		Set 3		Set 4		Set 5	
	Wt.	Rep	Wt.	Rep	Wt.	Rep	Wt.	Rep	Wt.	Rep

Comments:

Protein Intake | **Workout Rating** ★ ★ ★ ★ ★

Date:	Start Time:			Finish Time:					
Mo Tu We Th Fr Sa Su	Workout:			Weight:					

Exercises	Set 1		Set 2		Set 3		Set 4		Set 5	
	Wt.	Rep	Wt.	Rep	Wt.	Rep	Wt.	Rep	Wt.	Rep

Comments:

Protein Intake

Workout Rating ★ ★ ★ ★ ★

Date:	Start Time:		Finish Time:	
Mo Tu We Th Fr Sa Su	Workout:		Weight:	

Exercises	Set 1		Set 2		Set 3		Set 4		Set 5	
	Wt.	Rep	Wt.	Rep	Wt.	Rep	Wt.	Rep	Wt.	Rep

Comments:

Protein Intake

Workout Rating ★ ★ ★ ★ ★

Date:	Start Time:		Finish Time:	
Mo Tu We Th Fr Sa Su	Workout:		Weight:	

Exercises	Set 1		Set 2		Set 3		Set 4		Set 5	
	Wt.	Rep	Wt.	Rep	Wt.	Rep	Wt.	Rep	Wt.	Rep

Comments:

Protein Intake

Workout Rating ★ ★ ★ ★ ★

Date:	Start Time:		Finish Time:		
Mo Tu We Th Fr Sa Su	Workout:		Weight:		

Exercises	Set 1		Set 2		Set 3		Set 4		Set 5	
	Wt.	Rep	Wt.	Rep	Wt.	Rep	Wt.	Rep	Wt.	Rep

Comments:

Protein Intake

Workout Rating ★ ★ ★ ★ ★

Date:	Start Time:		Finish Time:	
Mo Tu We Th Fr Sa Su	Workout:		Weight:	

Exercises	Set 1		Set 2		Set 3		Set 4		Set 5	
	Wt.	Rep	Wt.	Rep	Wt.	Rep	Wt.	Rep	Wt.	Rep

Comments:

Protein Intake | **Workout Rating** ★ ★ ★ ★ ★

Date:	Start Time:		Finish Time:	
Mo Tu We Th Fr Sa Su	Workout:		Weight:	

Exercises	Set 1		Set 2		Set 3		Set 4		Set 5	
	Wt.	Rep	Wt.	Rep	Wt.	Rep	Wt.	Rep	Wt.	Rep

Comments:

Protein Intake

Workout Rating ★ ★ ★ ★ ★

Date:	Start Time:		Finish Time:	
Mo Tu We Th Fr Sa Su	Workout:		Weight:	

Exercises	Set 1		Set 2		Set 3		Set 4		Set 5	
	Wt.	Rep	Wt.	Rep	Wt.	Rep	Wt.	Rep	Wt.	Rep

Comments:

Protein Intake	**Workout Rating** ★ ★ ★ ★ ★

Date:	Start Time:			Finish Time:					
Mo Tu We Th Fr Sa Su	Workout:			Weight:					

Exercises	Set 1		Set 2		Set 3		Set 4		Set 5	
	Wt.	Rep	Wt.	Rep	Wt.	Rep	Wt.	Rep	Wt.	Rep

Comments:

Protein Intake

Workout Rating ★ ★ ★ ★ ★

Date:	Start Time:			Finish Time:					
Mo Tu We Th Fr Sa Su	Workout:			Weight:					

Exercises	Set 1		Set 2		Set 3		Set 4		Set 5	
	Wt.	Rep	Wt.	Rep	Wt.	Rep	Wt.	Rep	Wt.	Rep

Comments:

Protein Intake

Workout Rating ★ ★ ★ ★ ★

Date:	Start Time:			Finish Time:					
Mo Tu We Th Fr Sa Su	Workout:			Weight:					

Exercises	Set 1		Set 2		Set 3		Set 4		Set 5	
	Wt.	Rep	Wt.	Rep	Wt.	Rep	Wt.	Rep	Wt.	Rep

Comments:

Protein Intake

Workout Rating ★ ★ ★ ★ ★

Date:				Start Time:				Finish Time:		
Mo Tu We Th Fr Sa Su				Workout:				Weight:		

Exercises	Set 1		Set 2		Set 3		Set 4		Set 5	
	Wt.	Rep	Wt.	Rep	Wt.	Rep	Wt.	Rep	Wt.	Rep

Comments:

Protein Intake

Workout Rating ★ ★ ★ ★ ★

Date:	Start Time:					Finish Time:				
Mo Tu We Th Fr Sa Su	Workout:					Weight:				

Exercises	Set 1		Set 2		Set 3		Set 4		Set 5	
	Wt.	Rep	Wt.	Rep	Wt.	Rep	Wt.	Rep	Wt.	Rep

Comments:

Protein Intake | **Workout Rating** ★ ★ ★ ★ ★

Date:		Start Time:			Finish Time:				
Mo Tu We Th Fr Sa Su		Workout:			Weight:				

Exercises	Set 1		Set 2		Set 3		Set 4		Set 5	
	Wt.	Rep	Wt.	Rep	Wt.	Rep	Wt.	Rep	Wt.	Rep

Comments:

Protein Intake

Workout Rating ★ ★ ★ ★ ★

Date:	Start Time:			Finish Time:					
Mo Tu We Th Fr Sa Su	Workout:			Weight:					

Exercises	Set 1		Set 2		Set 3		Set 4		Set 5	
	Wt.	Rep	Wt.	Rep	Wt.	Rep	Wt.	Rep	Wt.	Rep

Comments:

Protein Intake

Workout Rating ★ ★ ★ ★ ★

Date:		Start Time:			Finish Time:				
Mo Tu We Th Fr Sa Su		Workout:			Weight:				

Exercises	Set 1		Set 2		Set 3		Set 4		Set 5	
	Wt.	Rep	Wt.	Rep	Wt.	Rep	Wt.	Rep	Wt.	Rep

Comments:

Protein Intake

Workout Rating ★ ★ ★ ★ ★

Date:	Start Time:		Finish Time:	
Mo Tu We Th Fr Sa Su	Workout:		Weight:	

Exercises	Set 1		Set 2		Set 3		Set 4		Set 5	
	Wt.	Rep	Wt.	Rep	Wt.	Rep	Wt.	Rep	Wt.	Rep

Comments:

Protein Intake

Workout Rating ★ ★ ★ ★ ★

Date:	Start Time:		Finish Time:	
Mo Tu We Th Fr Sa Su	Workout:		Weight:	

Exercises	Set 1		Set 2		Set 3		Set 4		Set 5	
	Wt.	Rep	Wt.	Rep	Wt.	Rep	Wt.	Rep	Wt.	Rep

Comments:

Protein Intake

Workout Rating ★ ★ ★ ★ ★

Date:	Start Time:		Finish Time:	
Mo Tu We Th Fr Sa Su	Workout:		Weight:	

Exercises	Set 1		Set 2		Set 3		Set 4		Set 5	
	Wt.	Rep	Wt.	Rep	Wt.	Rep	Wt.	Rep	Wt.	Rep

Comments:

Protein Intake

Workout Rating ★ ★ ★ ★

Date:	Start Time:		Finish Time:	
Mo Tu We Th Fr Sa Su	Workout:		Weight:	

Exercises	Set 1		Set 2		Set 3		Set 4		Set 5	
	Wt.	Rep	Wt.	Rep	Wt.	Rep	Wt.	Rep	Wt.	Rep

Comments:

Protein Intake

Workout Rating ★ ★ ★ ★ ★

Date:	Start Time:		Finish Time:	
Mo Tu We Th Fr Sa Su	Workout:		Weight:	

Exercises	Set 1		Set 2		Set 3		Set 4		Set 5	
	Wt.	Rep	Wt.	Rep	Wt.	Rep	Wt.	Rep	Wt.	Rep

Comments:

Protein Intake

Workout Rating ★ ★ ★ ★ ★

Date:	Start Time:		Finish Time:	
Mo Tu We Th Fr Sa Su	Workout:		Weight:	

Exercises	Set 1		Set 2		Set 3		Set 4		Set 5	
	Wt.	Rep	Wt.	Rep	Wt.	Rep	Wt.	Rep	Wt.	Rep

Comments:

Protein Intake

Workout Rating ★ ★ ★ ★ ★

Date:		Start Time:			Finish Time:				
Mo Tu We Th Fr Sa Su		Workout:			Weight:				

Exercises	Set 1		Set 2		Set 3		Set 4		Set 5	
	Wt.	Rep	Wt.	Rep	Wt.	Rep	Wt.	Rep	Wt.	Rep

Comments:

Protein Intake

Workout Rating ★ ★ ★ ★ ★

Date:				Start Time:				Finish Time:			
Mo Tu We Th Fr Sa Su				Workout:				Weight:			

Exercises	Set 1		Set 2		Set 3		Set 4		Set 5	
	Wt.	Rep	Wt.	Rep	Wt.	Rep	Wt.	Rep	Wt.	Rep

Comments:

Protein Intake | **Workout Rating** ★ ★ ★ ★ ★

Date:	Start Time:		Finish Time:	
Mo Tu We Th Fr Sa Su	Workout:		Weight:	

Exercises	Set 1		Set 2		Set 3		Set 4		Set 5	
	Wt.	Rep	Wt.	Rep	Wt.	Rep	Wt.	Rep	Wt.	Rep

Comments:

Protein Intake

Workout Rating ★ ★ ★ ★ ★

Date:			Start Time:				Finish Time:				
Mo Tu We Th Fr Sa Su			Workout:				Weight:				

Exercises	Set 1		Set 2		Set 3		Set 4		Set 5	
	Wt.	Rep	Wt.	Rep	Wt.	Rep	Wt.	Rep	Wt.	Rep

Comments:

Protein Intake

Workout Rating ★ ★ ★ ★ ★

Date:	Start Time:					Finish Time:				
Mo Tu We Th Fr Sa Su	Workout:					Weight:				

Exercises	Set 1		Set 2		Set 3		Set 4		Set 5	
	Wt.	Rep	Wt.	Rep	Wt.	Rep	Wt.	Rep	Wt.	Rep

Comments:

Protein Intake

Workout Rating ★ ★ ★ ★ ★

Date:	Start Time:		Finish Time:	
Mo Tu We Th Fr Sa Su	Workout:		Weight:	

Exercises	Set 1		Set 2		Set 3		Set 4		Set 5	
	Wt.	Rep	Wt.	Rep	Wt.	Rep	Wt.	Rep	Wt.	Rep

Comments:

Protein Intake

Workout Rating ★ ★ ★ ★ ★

Date:		Start Time:			Finish Time:		
Mo Tu We Th Fr Sa Su		Workout:			Weight:		

Exercises	Set 1		Set 2		Set 3		Set 4		Set 5	
	Wt.	Rep	Wt.	Rep	Wt.	Rep	Wt.	Rep	Wt.	Rep

Comments:

Protein Intake

Workout Rating ★ ★ ★ ★ ★

Date:	Start Time:		Finish Time:	
Mo Tu We Th Fr Sa Su	Workout:		Weight:	

Exercises	Set 1		Set 2		Set 3		Set 4		Set 5	
	Wt.	Rep	Wt.	Rep	Wt.	Rep	Wt.	Rep	Wt.	Rep

Comments:

Protein Intake

Workout Rating ★ ★ ★ ★ ★

Date:	Start Time:			Finish Time:					
Mo Tu We Th Fr Sa Su	Workout:			Weight:					

Exercises	Set 1		Set 2		Set 3		Set 4		Set 5	
	Wt.	Rep	Wt.	Rep	Wt.	Rep	Wt.	Rep	Wt.	Rep

Comments:

Protein Intake	Workout Rating ★ ★ ★ ★ ★

Date:		Start Time:			Finish Time:				
Mo Tu We Th Fr Sa Su		Workout:			Weight:				

Exercises	Set 1		Set 2		Set 3		Set 4		Set 5	
	Wt.	Rep	Wt.	Rep	Wt.	Rep	Wt.	Rep	Wt.	Rep

Comments:

Protein Intake

Workout Rating ★ ★ ★ ★ ★

Date:	Start Time:			Finish Time:					
Mo Tu We Th Fr Sa Su	Workout:			Weight:					

Exercises	Set 1		Set 2		Set 3		Set 4		Set 5	
	Wt.	Rep	Wt.	Rep	Wt.	Rep	Wt.	Rep	Wt.	Rep

Comments:

Protein Intake

Workout Rating ★ ★ ★ ★ ★

Date:			Start Time:			Finish Time:		
Mo Tu We Th Fr Sa Su			Workout:			Weight:		

Exercises	Set 1		Set 2		Set 3		Set 4		Set 5	
	Wt.	Rep	Wt.	Rep	Wt.	Rep	Wt.	Rep	Wt.	Rep

Comments:

Protein Intake

Workout Rating ★ ★ ★ ★ ★

Date:	Start Time:		Finish Time:	
Mo Tu We Th Fr Sa Su	Workout:		Weight:	

Exercises	Set 1		Set 2		Set 3		Set 4		Set 5	
	Wt.	Rep	Wt.	Rep	Wt.	Rep	Wt.	Rep	Wt.	Rep

Comments:

Protein Intake

Workout Rating ★ ★ ★ ★ ★

Date:	Start Time:			Finish Time:					
Mo Tu We Th Fr Sa Su	Workout:			Weight:					

Exercises	Set 1		Set 2		Set 3		Set 4		Set 5	
	Wt.	Rep	Wt.	Rep	Wt.	Rep	Wt.	Rep	Wt.	Rep

Comments:

Protein Intake

Workout Rating ★ ★ ★ ★ ★

Date:	Start Time:							Finish Time:		
Mo Tu We Th Fr Sa Su	Workout:							Weight:		

Exercises	Set 1		Set 2		Set 3		Set 4		Set 5	
	Wt.	Rep	Wt.	Rep	Wt.	Rep	Wt.	Rep	Wt.	Rep

Comments:

Protein Intake

Workout Rating ★ ★ ★ ★ ★

Date:	Start Time:		Finish Time:	
Mo Tu We Th Fr Sa Su	Workout:		Weight:	

Exercises	Set 1		Set 2		Set 3		Set 4		Set 5	
	Wt.	Rep	Wt.	Rep	Wt.	Rep	Wt.	Rep	Wt.	Rep

Comments:

Protein Intake

Workout Rating ★ ★ ★ ★ ★

Date:	Start Time:					Finish Time:				
Mo Tu We Th Fr Sa Su	Workout:					Weight:				

Exercises	Set 1		Set 2		Set 3		Set 4		Set 5	
	Wt.	Rep	Wt.	Rep	Wt.	Rep	Wt.	Rep	Wt.	Rep

Comments:

Protein Intake

Workout Rating ★ ★ ★ ★ ★

Date:			Start Time:			Finish Time:				
Mo Tu We Th Fr Sa Su			Workout:			Weight:				

Exercises	Set 1		Set 2		Set 3		Set 4		Set 5	
	Wt.	Rep	Wt.	Rep	Wt.	Rep	Wt.	Rep	Wt.	Rep

Comments:

Protein Intake

Workout Rating ★ ★ ★ ★ ★

Date:	Start Time:		Finish Time:	
Mo Tu We Th Fr Sa Su	Workout:		Weight:	

Exercises	Set 1		Set 2		Set 3		Set 4		Set 5	
	Wt.	Rep	Wt.	Rep	Wt.	Rep	Wt.	Rep	Wt.	Rep

Comments:

Protein Intake

Workout Rating ★ ★ ★ ★ ★

Date:	Start Time:		Finish Time:	
Mo Tu We Th Fr Sa Su	Workout:		Weight:	

Exercises	Set 1		Set 2		Set 3		Set 4		Set 5	
	Wt.	Rep	Wt.	Rep	Wt.	Rep	Wt.	Rep	Wt.	Rep

Comments:

Protein Intake	Workout Rating ★ ★ ★ ★ ★

Date:	Start Time:		Finish Time:	
Mo Tu We Th Fr Sa Su	Workout:		Weight:	

Exercises	Set 1		Set 2		Set 3		Set 4		Set 5	
	Wt.	Rep	Wt.	Rep	Wt.	Rep	Wt.	Rep	Wt.	Rep

Comments:

Protein Intake

Workout Rating ★ ★ ★ ★ ★

Date:				Start Time:		Finish Time:			
Mo Tu We Th Fr Sa Su				Workout:		Weight:			

Exercises	Set 1		Set 2		Set 3		Set 4		Set 5	
	Wt.	Rep	Wt.	Rep	Wt.	Rep	Wt.	Rep	Wt.	Rep

Comments:

Protein Intake

Workout Rating ★ ★ ★ ★ ★

Date:	Start Time:		Finish Time:	
Mo Tu We Th Fr Sa Su	Workout:		Weight:	

Exercises	Set 1		Set 2		Set 3		Set 4		Set 5	
	Wt.	Rep	Wt.	Rep	Wt.	Rep	Wt.	Rep	Wt.	Rep

Comments:

Protein Intake

Workout Rating ★ ★ ★ ★ ★

Date:		Start Time:			Finish Time:				
Mo Tu We Th Fr Sa Su		Workout:			Weight:				

Exercises	Set 1		Set 2		Set 3		Set 4		Set 5	
	Wt.	Rep	Wt.	Rep	Wt.	Rep	Wt.	Rep	Wt.	Rep

Comments:

Protein Intake

Workout Rating ★ ★ ★ ★ ★

Date:	Start Time:		Finish Time:	
Mo Tu We Th Fr Sa Su	Workout:		Weight:	

Exercises	Set 1		Set 2		Set 3		Set 4		Set 5	
	Wt.	Rep	Wt.	Rep	Wt.	Rep	Wt.	Rep	Wt.	Rep

Comments:

Protein Intake

Workout Rating ★ ★ ★ ★ ★

Date:	Start Time:			Finish Time:					
Mo Tu We Th Fr Sa Su	Workout:			Weight:					

Exercises	Set 1		Set 2		Set 3		Set 4		Set 5	
	Wt.	Rep	Wt.	Rep	Wt.	Rep	Wt.	Rep	Wt.	Rep

Comments:

Protein Intake

Workout Rating ★ ★ ★ ★ ★

Date:	Start Time:		Finish Time:	
Mo Tu We Th Fr Sa Su	Workout:		Weight:	

Exercises	Set 1		Set 2		Set 3		Set 4		Set 5	
	Wt.	Rep	Wt.	Rep	Wt.	Rep	Wt.	Rep	Wt.	Rep

Comments:

Protein Intake

Workout Rating ★ ★ ★ ★ ★

Date:	Start Time:		Finish Time:	
Mo Tu We Th Fr Sa Su	Workout:		Weight:	

Exercises	Set 1		Set 2		Set 3		Set 4		Set 5	
	Wt.	Rep	Wt.	Rep	Wt.	Rep	Wt.	Rep	Wt.	Rep

Comments:

Protein Intake

Workout Rating ★ ★ ★ ★ ★

Date:	Start Time:			Finish Time:		
Mo Tu We Th Fr Sa Su	Workout:			Weight:		

Exercises	Set 1		Set 2		Set 3		Set 4		Set 5	
	Wt.	Rep	Wt.	Rep	Wt.	Rep	Wt.	Rep	Wt.	Rep

Comments:

Protein Intake

Workout Rating ★ ★ ★ ★ ★

Date:		Start Time:			Finish Time:				
Mo Tu We Th Fr Sa Su		Workout:			Weight:				

Exercises	Set 1		Set 2		Set 3		Set 4		Set 5	
	Wt.	Rep	Wt.	Rep	Wt.	Rep	Wt.	Rep	Wt.	Rep

Comments:

Protein Intake

Workout Rating ★ ★ ★ ★ ★

Date:	Start Time:		Finish Time:	
Mo Tu We Th Fr Sa Su	Workout:		Weight:	

Exercises	Set 1		Set 2		Set 3		Set 4		Set 5	
	Wt.	Rep	Wt.	Rep	Wt.	Rep	Wt.	Rep	Wt.	Rep

Comments:

Protein Intake

Workout Rating ★ ★ ★ ★ ★

Date:	Start Time:		Finish Time:		
Mo Tu We Th Fr Sa Su	Workout:		Weight:		

Exercises	Set 1		Set 2		Set 3		Set 4		Set 5	
	Wt.	Rep	Wt.	Rep	Wt.	Rep	Wt.	Rep	Wt.	Rep

Comments:

Protein Intake

Workout Rating ★ ★ ★ ★ ★

Date:	Start Time:				Finish Time:				
Mo Tu We Th Fr Sa Su	Workout:				Weight:				

Exercises	Set 1		Set 2		Set 3		Set 4		Set 5	
	Wt.	Rep	Wt.	Rep	Wt.	Rep	Wt.	Rep	Wt.	Rep

Comments:

Protein Intake

Workout Rating ★ ★ ★ ★ ★

Date:	Start Time:		Finish Time:	
Mo Tu We Th Fr Sa Su	Workout:		Weight:	

Exercises	Set 1		Set 2		Set 3		Set 4		Set 5	
	Wt.	Rep	Wt.	Rep	Wt.	Rep	Wt.	Rep	Wt.	Rep

Comments:

Protein Intake | **Workout Rating** ★ ★ ★ ★ ★

Date:	Start Time:		Finish Time:							
Mo Tu We Th Fr Sa Su	Workout:		Weight:							
Exercises	Set 1		Set 2		Set 3		Set 4		Set 5	
	Wt.	Rep	Wt.	Rep	Wt.	Rep	Wt.	Rep	Wt.	Rep

Comments:

Protein Intake

Workout Rating ★ ★ ★ ★ ★

Date:	Start Time:			Finish Time:					
Mo Tu We Th Fr Sa Su	Workout:			Weight:					

Exercises	Set 1		Set 2		Set 3		Set 4		Set 5	
	Wt.	Rep	Wt.	Rep	Wt.	Rep	Wt.	Rep	Wt.	Rep

Comments:

Protein Intake

Workout Rating ★ ★ ★ ★ ★

Date:	Start Time:		Finish Time:	
Mo Tu We Th Fr Sa Su	Workout:		Weight:	

Exercises	Set 1		Set 2		Set 3		Set 4		Set 5	
	Wt.	Rep	Wt.	Rep	Wt.	Rep	Wt.	Rep	Wt.	Rep

Comments:

Protein Intake

Workout Rating ★ ★ ★ ★ ★

Date:	Start Time:			Finish Time:				
Mo Tu We Th Fr Sa Su	Workout:			Weight:				

Exercises	Set 1		Set 2		Set 3		Set 4		Set 5	
	Wt.	Rep	Wt.	Rep	Wt.	Rep	Wt.	Rep	Wt.	Rep

Comments:

Protein Intake   **Workout Rating** ★ ★ ★ ★ ★

Date:	Start Time:		Finish Time:		
Mo Tu We Th Fr Sa Su	Workout:		Weight:		

Exercises	Set 1		Set 2		Set 3		Set 4		Set 5	
	Wt.	Rep	Wt.	Rep	Wt.	Rep	Wt.	Rep	Wt.	Rep

Comments:

Protein Intake

Workout Rating ★ ★ ★ ★ ★

Date:	Start Time:					Finish Time:				
Mo Tu We Th Fr Sa Su	Workout:					Weight:				

Exercises	Set 1		Set 2		Set 3		Set 4		Set 5	
	Wt.	Rep	Wt.	Rep	Wt.	Rep	Wt.	Rep	Wt.	Rep

Comments:

Protein Intake

Workout Rating ★ ★ ★ ★ ★

Date:		Start Time:			Finish Time:			
Mo Tu We Th Fr Sa Su		Workout:			Weight:			

Exercises	Set 1		Set 2		Set 3		Set 4		Set 5	
	Wt.	Rep	Wt.	Rep	Wt.	Rep	Wt.	Rep	Wt.	Rep

Comments:

Protein Intake

Workout Rating ★ ★ ★ ★ ★

Date:	Start Time:						Finish Time:				
Mo Tu We Th Fr Sa Su	Workout:						Weight:				
Exercises	Set 1		Set 2		Set 3		Set 4		Set 5	
	Wt.	Rep	Wt.	Rep	Wt.	Rep	Wt.	Rep	Wt.	Rep

Comments:

Protein Intake

Workout Rating ★ ★ ★ ★ ★

Date:	Start Time:					Finish Time:				
Mo Tu We Th Fr Sa Su	Workout:					Weight:				

Exercises	Set 1		Set 2		Set 3		Set 4		Set 5	
	Wt.	Rep	Wt.	Rep	Wt.	Rep	Wt.	Rep	Wt.	Rep

Comments:

Protein Intake

Workout Rating ★ ★ ★ ★ ★

Date:		Start Time:			Finish Time:				
Mo Tu We Th Fr Sa Su		Workout:			Weight:				

Exercises	Set 1		Set 2		Set 3		Set 4		Set 5	
	Wt.	Rep	Wt.	Rep	Wt.	Rep	Wt.	Rep	Wt.	Rep

Comments:

Protein Intake

Workout Rating ★ ★ ★ ★ ★

Date:	Start Time:	Finish Time:
Mo Tu We Th Fr Sa Su	Workout:	Weight:

Exercises	Set 1		Set 2		Set 3		Set 4		Set 5	
	Wt.	Rep	Wt.	Rep	Wt.	Rep	Wt.	Rep	Wt.	Rep

Comments:

Protein Intake

Workout Rating ★ ★ ★ ★ ★

Date:	Start Time:				Finish Time:				
Mo Tu We Th Fr Sa Su	Workout:				Weight:				

Exercises	Set 1		Set 2		Set 3		Set 4		Set 5	
	Wt.	Rep	Wt.	Rep	Wt.	Rep	Wt.	Rep	Wt.	Rep

Comments:

Protein Intake

Workout Rating ★ ★ ★ ★ ★

Date:	Start Time:					Finish Time:				
Mo Tu We Th Fr Sa Su	Workout:					Weight:				

Exercises	Set 1		Set 2		Set 3		Set 4		Set 5	
	Wt.	Rep	Wt.	Rep	Wt.	Rep	Wt.	Rep	Wt.	Rep

Comments:

Protein Intake

Workout Rating ★ ★ ★ ★ ★

Date:	Start Time:		Finish Time:	
Mo Tu We Th Fr Sa Su	Workout:		Weight:	

Exercises	Set 1		Set 2		Set 3		Set 4		Set 5	
	Wt.	Rep	Wt.	Rep	Wt.	Rep	Wt.	Rep	Wt.	Rep

Comments:

Protein Intake

Workout Rating ★ ★ ★ ★ ★

Date:	Start Time:					Finish Time:				
Mo Tu We Th Fr Sa Su	Workout:					Weight:				

Exercises	Set 1		Set 2		Set 3		Set 4		Set 5	
	Wt.	Rep	Wt.	Rep	Wt.	Rep	Wt.	Rep	Wt.	Rep

Comments:

Protein Intake

Workout Rating ★ ★ ★ ★ ★

Date:	Start Time:			Finish Time:		
Mo Tu We Th Fr Sa Su	Workout:			Weight:		

Exercises	Set 1		Set 2		Set 3		Set 4		Set 5	
	Wt.	Rep	Wt.	Rep	Wt.	Rep	Wt.	Rep	Wt.	Rep

Comments:

Protein Intake

Workout Rating ★ ★ ★ ★ ★

Date:	Start Time:					Finish Time:				
Mo Tu We Th Fr Sa Su	Workout:					Weight:				

Exercises	Set 1		Set 2		Set 3		Set 4		Set 5	
	Wt.	Rep	Wt.	Rep	Wt.	Rep	Wt.	Rep	Wt.	Rep

Comments:

Protein Intake

Workout Rating ★ ★ ★ ★ ★

Date:			Start Time:				Finish Time:		
Mo Tu We Th Fr Sa Su			Workout:				Weight:		

Exercises	Set 1		Set 2		Set 3		Set 4		Set 5	
	Wt.	Rep	Wt.	Rep	Wt.	Rep	Wt.	Rep	Wt.	Rep

Comments:

Protein Intake

Workout Rating ★ ★ ★ ★ ★

Date:	Start Time:		Finish Time:	
Mo Tu We Th Fr Sa Su	Workout:		Weight:	

Exercises	Set 1		Set 2		Set 3		Set 4		Set 5	
	Wt.	Rep	Wt.	Rep	Wt.	Rep	Wt.	Rep	Wt.	Rep

Comments:

Protein Intake

Workout Rating ★ ★ ★ ★ ★

Date:	Start Time:		Finish Time:	
Mo Tu We Th Fr Sa Su	Workout:		Weight:	

Exercises	Set 1		Set 2		Set 3		Set 4		Set 5	
	Wt.	Rep	Wt.	Rep	Wt.	Rep	Wt.	Rep	Wt.	Rep

Comments:

Protein Intake

Workout Rating ★ ★ ★ ★ ★

Date:	Start Time:		Finish Time:	
Mo Tu We Th Fr Sa Su	Workout:		Weight:	

Exercises	Set 1		Set 2		Set 3		Set 4		Set 5	
	Wt.	Rep	Wt.	Rep	Wt.	Rep	Wt.	Rep	Wt.	Rep

Comments:

Protein Intake

Workout Rating ★ ★ ★ ★ ★

Date:	Start Time:		Finish Time:	
Mo Tu We Th Fr Sa Su	Workout:		Weight:	

Exercises	Set 1		Set 2		Set 3		Set 4		Set 5	
	Wt.	Rep	Wt.	Rep	Wt.	Rep	Wt.	Rep	Wt.	Rep

Comments:

Protein Intake

Workout Rating ★ ★ ★ ★ ★

Date:	Start Time:		Finish Time:	
Mo Tu We Th Fr Sa Su	Workout:		Weight:	

Exercises	Set 1		Set 2		Set 3		Set 4		Set 5	
	Wt.	Rep	Wt.	Rep	Wt.	Rep	Wt.	Rep	Wt.	Rep

Comments:

Protein Intake

Workout Rating ★ ★ ★ ★ ★

Date:	Start Time:		Finish Time:	
Mo Tu We Th Fr Sa Su	Workout:		Weight:	

Exercises	Set 1		Set 2		Set 3		Set 4		Set 5	
	Wt.	Rep	Wt.	Rep	Wt.	Rep	Wt.	Rep	Wt.	Rep

Comments:

Protein Intake

Workout Rating ★ ★ ★ ★ ★

Date:	Start Time:					Finish Time:				
Mo Tu We Th Fr Sa Su	Workout:					Weight:				

Exercises	Set 1		Set 2		Set 3		Set 4		Set 5	
	Wt.	Rep	Wt.	Rep	Wt.	Rep	Wt.	Rep	Wt.	Rep

Comments:

Protein Intake

Workout Rating ★ ★ ★ ★ ★

Month:

Sunday	Monday	Tuesday	Wednesday	Thursday	Friday	Saturday
☐	☐	☐	☐	☐	☐	☐
☐	☐	☐	☐	☐	☐	☐
☐	☐	☐	☐	☐	☐	☐
☐	☐	☐	☐	☐	☐	☐
☐	☐	☐	☐	☐	☐	☐
☐	☐	Notes:				

Month:

Sunday	Monday	Tuesday	Wednesday	Thursday	Friday	Saturday
☐	☐	☐	☐	☐	☐	☐
☐	☐	☐	☐	☐	☐	☐
☐	☐	☐	☐	☐	☐	☐
☐	☐	☐	☐	☐	☐	☐
☐	☐	☐	☐	☐	☐	☐
☐	☐	Notes:				

Month:

Sunday	Monday	Tuesday	Wednesday	Thursday	Friday	Saturday
☐	☐	☐	☐	☐	☐	☐
☐	☐	☐	☐	☐	☐	☐
☐	☐	☐	☐	☐	☐	☐
☐	☐	☐	☐	☐	☐	☐
☐	☐	☐	☐	☐	☐	☐
☐	☐					

Notes:

Month:

Sunday	Monday	Tuesday	Wednesday	Thursday	Friday	Saturday
☐	☐	☐	☐	☐	☐	☐
☐	☐	☐	☐	☐	☐	☐
☐	☐	☐	☐	☐	☐	☐
☐	☐	☐	☐	☐	☐	☐
☐	☐	☐	☐	☐	☐	☐
☐	☐	Notes:				

Notes

Notes

Printed in Great Britain
by Amazon